Roadmap to Rich

Roadmap to Riches on $ 12.50 Per Week is just the ticket for women in transition who are stepping out into the workforce and need to know how to manage their money. Ms. Whitley presents basic principles about money, savings and investments in a way that is not intimidating but quite the opposite—it is friendly and engaging. Perfect for the woman who is just starting out.

Jill Miller
Executive Director
Women Work! The National Network for Women's Employment
Washington, DC

The most useful book I've ever edited.

Vera Webster
President (Ret.)
Advances in Instruction
A Division of Hartcourt Brace Jovanovich
New York, NY

I think this book provides excellent information. Writing a useful book is a tremendous public service. I wish you much success.

Senator Ed Warren
NC Legislature (Ret.)

I read your book and loved it. It was nice to read a book for novices that doesn't get bogged down in details so you can actually remember what you've learned.

Jack Blumenfeld
Attorney
Wilmington, Delaware

The book's chief contribution, aside from the really good practical information it contains, may be to de-mystify the world of investing and simultaneously bring levity and joy to an important area of life that so many people are made to feel incompetent to handle. I don't think I have ever before laughed out loud while reading a book on investing money!

Dr. Charles Coble
Vice President (Ret.)
Center Education Commission of the States
Denver, Colorado

Once I started reading this book, I could not put it down. Due to its simple approach to financial management, I highly recommend the book to everyone, especially young adults.

Ann Brown
National Sales Director
Mary Kay Cosmetics, Inc.

Roadmap to Riches on $12.50 Per Week is a wonderful book - what a great way to learn about personal finances. I wish we could offer the information covered in your book to every high school senior in North Carolina. Thank you for sharing your knowledge and experience.

Kathy A. Taft
NC State Board of Education
Educators Hall of Fame
East Carolina University College of Education

I read this delightful book with pleasure. Life is filled with abundance. Thank you for your practical and spiritual points on how to create them for ourselves.

Janice Faulkner
NC Commissioner (Ret.)
Division of Motor Vehicles

This is a wonderful book of easy to understand, practical information for financial investing...a must read for young adults just beginning their careers.

Susanne D. Sartelle, CCE
President
Greenville-Pitt County Chamber of Commerce

Finally a book that enables young people to move forward and become millionaires.

Terry Shank
Former Pitt County Commissioner and
School Board Member

Roadmap to Riches on $12.50 Per Week was the first book I've read since high school. It surprised me to learn that such a small amount of money put away each week could be such a big benefit to my son in the future. Thank you.

Terry Raper
Flo's Kitchen
Wilson, NC

When I first read Donna Whitley's book *Roadmap to Riches on $12.50 Per Week: First Steps to Financial Freedom*, I was "mad as fire" because I was looking for a get rich fast way, and I had wasted my money buying the book. But I decided to go ahead and start putting the $12.50 per week in a savings account. Before too long I realized I could do better than $12.50 and so gradually put more and more into savings. After about a year I lost my job and went to the bank to find out how much money was in the account. What a shock – it was so much more money than I expected I almost "fell on the floor." I lived off that money for several months until I got another job.

It was at this point I enthusiastically embraced Donna's ideas and started saving with a passion. I had a dream. My goal was to own a Christian Radio Station. As of February 1, 2005, I am proudly leasing a Christian Gospel Radio Station in Washington, NC 1320 AM with plans to buy! She has been an inspiration to me!

Mae Rogers
903 Hackney Avenue
Washington, NC 27889

You have changed my life! I have a total different relationship with money.

Robin Adams
Dorcas Place Adult & Family Learning Center
220 Elmwood Avenue
Providence, Rhode Island 02906

Ms. Whitley's gift is to take a complicated subject matter – finances – and transform it into a fascinating and fun learning experience. We look forward to her returning to our campus.

Margaret-Ann Radford-Wedemeyer
Associate Dean of College Life
Gettysburg College, Gettysburg, PA

FINALLY, a book about personal finance that offers a clear path to success for people who don't have professional money managers. *Roadmap to Riches on $12.50 Per Week* is a sound investment in your financial future.

Ann Blackman
Author
Wild Rose, Civil War Spy
Washington, DC

It is a pleasure to recommend for your consideration the skillful, effective presentation skills of Donna Whitley, who recently spoke to my math classes about compound interest and financial planning...her winning personality and friendly, southern manner made her an instant hit..

Matthew P. Cate
Casablanca American School, Morocco

ROADMAP TO RICHES ON $12.50 PER WEEK

FIRST STEPS TO FINANCIAL FREEDOM

Donna Whitley

To the Evans Family, with love and respect, Donna Whitley

Roadmap to Riches on $12.50 Per Week
First Steps to Financial Freedom
Copyright © 2002 by Donna Whitley
Printed Acculink 2006

All rights reserved. No part of this publication may be reproduced, stored in a retrieval system, or transmitted in any form or by any means - electronic, mechanical, photocopy, recording, or any other - except for brief quotations in printed reviews, without the prior permission of the publisher.

Cover and book design by Carolyn Whitley.

For information, please contact:
WS Productions
Donna Whitley
1800 Forest Hill Drive
Greenville, North Carolina 27858

ISBN 0-9725866-0-1

Dedication

This book is lovingly dedicated to
Kacem, Farah Lisa, Adam,
and my "belle soeur" Carolyn

Acknowledgments

Many friends helped me to transform these ideas into a book. I thank them from the bottom of my heart. Without their love and support, I could not have created this fun book.
Mary Earle Chase, Annette Brooks, Mark Jones, Abbott Morris, George Sappenfield, Paula Blumenfeld, Joe Gantz, Sissy Gamble, Peter Lichstein, Martha Henderson, Carl Henley, Senator Ed Warren, Irene O'Boyle, Charlie Coble, Terry Shank, Bryan Whitley, Jonathan Whitley, Amaya, Lisa Blakeslee, Kay Tyndall Rowe and Landmark Education.
Special thanks to my "belle soeur" Carolyn Whitley who designed the layout and spent many nights typing this book.
Vera Webster, an angel, edited the copy and guided us in the arcane art of preparing a book for publication.

CONTENTS

INTRODUCTION

Chapter One: What Is The Golden Rule Of Financial Independence?
PAY YOURSELF FIRST
- 1 -

Chapter Two: What Is The Eighth Wonder Of The World?
COMPOUND INTEREST
- 19 -

Chapter Three: Where Do I Put My Money So It Can Grow?
MUTUAL FUNDS
- 30 -

Chapter Four: What Is Dollar Cost Averaging?
CONSISTENCY IS THE KEY TO SUCCESS
- 48 -

Chapter Five: What Is The Silent Thief?
INFLATION
- 55 -

Chapter Six: What Is Diversification?
DO NOT PUT ALL YOUR EGGS
IN ONE BASKET
- 61 -
Chapter Seven: Who Can Help Me
Put It All Together?
HOW TO CHOOSE A FINANCIAL
PLANNER
- 68 -
Chapter Eight: How Can I Change My Attitude
Toward Money?
QUOTES TO LIVE BY
- 75 -
Chapter Nine: What Are Some Simple
Practical Tips For Life?
SIMPLE AND IMPORTANT
THINGS TO KNOW
- 81 -
Chapter Ten: What Do I Do Now? Homework!
A THOUSAND MILE JOURNEY
BEGINS WITH ONE STEP!
- 88 -
CONCLUSION
- 95 -
GLOSSARY
- 106 -

Introduction

"Water, water everywhere and not a drop to drink."

In the bookstore standing before the shelves stacked with books about finances, those words sang In my mind. I leafed through the books overwhelmed by graphs, charts, and the sheer number of words and pages.

Why can't someone write a simple-easy-to-read and fun book about how to take charge of your finances? Since it did not exist, it took me two years of wading through volumes of Information, plus attending classes to get started on my journey to financial independence.

What started me on my road to financial independence? In 1990 our family was in debt and neither my husband Kacem nor I could balance a checkbook. Kacem was a sculptor and worked as a fire fighter. I was a stay-at-home Mom working part-time teaching bellydance and selling Mary Kay Cosmetics. In a couple of years Farah Lisa and Adam were ready for college and no plans had been made. No thoughts had been given to funding future wedding celebrations. But, the one piece of information that catapulted me into action was discovering that Kacem's retirement benefits in 2003 would not be enough to live on. In addition, I would have to pay $350.00 per month to be included in his health care policy. We were in a mess.

How had I gotten into this quandary? College educated and reasonably intelligent, I had married into a prominent Moroccan family. My expectation had been that marriage to a college graduate from a good family equalled financial security. What went wrong? I didn't know. So after torturing myself for months about how awful the situation was, I gave up that Prince Charming was going to rescue me and resentfully headed for the library.

My journey to financial power and independence began on a rainy afternoon in the public library. It would be two years and thousands of pages later before I was able to do anything. The first months were devoted to learning the theories of how to become financially solvent. It took a long time before I had the courage to hand my hard-earned money over to an investment group to manage it for me. When I did, $12.50 a week was all I could muster.

Barbara Stanny's <u>Prince Charming Isn't Coming</u> tells her story - the H&R Block heiress whose husband spent her fortune, and she was forced to create one for herself. The story of women facing the financial dragon and piercing it to the heart with their knowledge is now commonplace. We women are speaking out and sharing our stories. Each story inspires another woman. We can speak with pride and say. "We did it. We left behind our fear and inadequacies. We embraced our intelligence and common sense to create ourselves as financial warriors." Let me tell you, it is a great place to be.

Read on with complete assurance that you are a financial warrior. After years of teaching complicated bellydance movements, teaching you to take charge of your life by taking charge of your money is as easy as teaching you to shimmy.

I started teaching Money 101: A Breakthrough Seminar for Women at the request of my bellydance students. They came to my studio to shimmy and undulate but also wanted to learn about finances. "Please organize your money knowledge into a separate class, and we will pay you to teach us how to become a Financial Warrior. But, let's dance during bellydance class!"

So I did. The way I approached developing the seminar was to read over my many spiral notebooks. I learned many interesting bits of information about financial independence. However, the eight points discussed in my course, which became this book, are the empowering concepts that redirected my life. Knowledge is power. My later years will be much more financially secure and comfortable than if I had never learned this information. My children can be millionaires and retire early if they choose to use this knowledge.

Years have passed. The children have graduated and are out in the world. Now is the time to write the simple-easy-to-read and fun book about finances.

P.S.
YOU could have figured this out for yourself if you had taken the time to read and study all the books I've read. The major points are in ALL THE BOOKS, BUT NOT LISTED ON THE FIRST PAGE. Think of me as your book reviewer and take to heart these points. They have the power to transform your life. Have fun, enjoy, and grow powerful.

… Is The Golden Rule Of
Financial Independence?

PAY YOURSELF FIRST

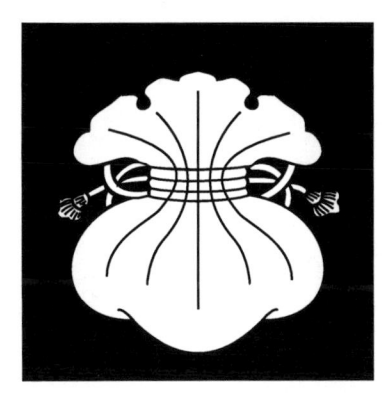

Chapter One

What is the Golden Rule of Financial Independence?

What is the difference between
SAVING AND PAYING YOURSELF FIRST?

Savings is money you put aside when the mortgage, utilities, groceries, insurance, car, and entertainment have been paid. It is usually not much money or nothing at all!

Paying yourself first means that YOU are the first payment on your list of bills each month!

Do you have $12.50 per week to set aside for your future?

Are you willing to take out $12.50 each week before you spend anything on rent, food, clothing, insurance, car payments, or entertainment? If the answer is "yes," read on. I can teach you how to begin the journey starting today to create financial independence. You can make many mistakes in life, (blow your inheritance, buy an expensive car, try to live beyond your means)

Pay Yourself First

but if you consistently each month invest in a respectable mutual fund, you will be able to have financial comfort long before you ever dreamed.

Pay yourself first is the secret to financial independence. The most painless way to do this is an automatic deduction by your employer so that you never see the money in your checking account.

If you are self-employed, arrange for the bank to act like your employer and transfer the money each month directly into a mutual fund.

This money, whether $12.50 per week or $125.00 per week, will create financial security if you invest it wisely and consistently.

This "off the top" money is invested for long term. I define long term as 10-20-30 years. The minimum definition of long term is 10 years. This is the only way a small amount of money can generate into large amounts of money.

What is the Golden Rule of Financial Independence?

A Magic of Compounding Story

At age 20 Tim and Tom graduated from college. Tim contributed $2,000 a year to his Individual Retirement Account (IRA) for the next 10 years (a total of $20,000). He never put another penny in it.

Tom did not contribute any money to his IRA until he was 30 years of age. For the next 35 years, he contributed $2,000 a year (a total of $70,000).

Who do you think had more money at the age of 65?

Based on a 9% annual rate of return, Tim who had contributed only $20,000 had $676,122.00 and Tom who had contributed $70,000 had $470,249.00.

The earlier you start investing, the better!

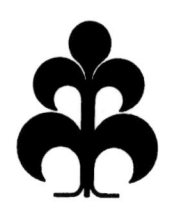

THE IDEAL SITUATION #1
PAY YOURSELF 10% OF YOUR EARNINGS

Isn't it amazing to realize that in ten years you will have saved one year's salary?

Begin today with $12.50 per week ($50.00 per month), watch it grow, and you will be inspired to do more.

REMEMBER: $12.50 per week ($50.00 per month) invested in the stock market for thirty years at 9% will yield you $91,537.

REMEMBER: $125.00 per week ($500.00 per month) invested in the stock market for thirty years at 9% will yield you $915,372.

IF YOU CAN'T AFFORD 10% OF YOUR SALARY, START WITH $12.50 PER WEEK AND ADD TO IT AS YOU CAN.

THE IDEAL SITUATION #2
CONTRIBUTE 10% TO A RELIGIOUS ORGANIZATION OR CHARITY

One intriguing jewel of information I discovered in my journey is the role of generosity. People who generate money and are comfortable with money give away money. It seems to be a top priority among religions that giving money to help people create a better world in this lifetime is an important discipline. Generosity releases a creative energy within the giver that in turn inspires them to generate more money or manage better the money they have.

There is a law of gratitude that works in the world. When we give generously, it shows that we trust the Divine Creator and that all is well. And if we use our talents which God has so generously bestowed upon us, all is well.

Stories from Hindus, Jews, Christians, Moslems, agnostics, and atheists verify this principle. You cannot generate money and a feeling of abundance with a clenched fist. The hands must be open and giving money away and ready to gently hold the money that is coming. Learning each day of my life to be generous with money is a continuous challenge for me. There have been moments I have experienced a sweetness, joy, and lightness of heart when giving money away. It is a feeling I want to experience more and more.

Mary Kay Ash, founder of Mary Kay Cosmetics and the Mary Kay Ash Charitable Foundation, shared this story in her autobiography. Her church was engaged in a money-raising campaign for a children's Sunday School building. Each week the congregation contributed $600 to $1000 toward the building fund. One Sunday Mary Kay decided to offer a stimulus; she would match dollar for dollar cash contributions until five o'clock. At the end of the time, the minister called and said, "Mary Kay, let me say right in the beginning, we do not hold you to your pledge. We have received $107,748!" Mary Kay did not despair. She looked at the commitment as one more challenge in life. Within a few days, one of her investments in a seismic technique for finding oil provided the $100,000 she had committed.

THE IDEAL SITUATION #3
SEPARATE ACCOUNTS

A. FOR LONG TERM GOALS:

In order to track the money you generate when you embrace the principle "Pay Yourself First," you will need separate accounts. One account is for your FUTURE FINANCIAL INDEPENDENCE AND SECURITY. This is sacred money invested for the future and it is <u>never</u> to be touched during that time period. Because of tax advantages, Individual Retirement Accounts (IRA) and 401K Retirement Accounts are very important separate accounts set up for the long term. You may choose to set up other long term accounts for dream goals, but the IRA and 401K are the foundation bricks in building your future financial independence and security.

B. FOR SHORT TERM GOALS:

Do you want to put money aside for a car, travel, house or education? Then it is necessary to set up separate accounts for each item. Why so many accounts? People will do better if they do not mix their money in one pot. It is much easier to track your progress if the money is in separate pots i.e. accounts. The principle applies to both long-term investments and short-term savings.

My friend and I flew to Charlotte NC to attend a seminar called "More Money," and as my husband said, we spent more money. The seminar leader directed us to return home and set up five to seven savings accounts and one checking before we returned the next week. We grumbled and complained, but he insisted it was a critical part of the education for which we were paying him quite handsomely. At our next session, he revealed the theory.

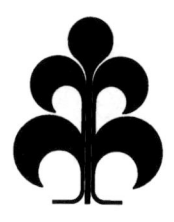

A high school friend contributed his Separate Account story. The only time he has ever borrowed money to buy an automobile was for his first one. When the car payments ended, he continued to write the check each month and deposited it in his Car Account. Why? He wanted to avoid paying the interest for borrowing money the next time he chose to buy a car. He believes that once in the habit of writing a car payment check each month, it is better to continue and pretend you have a car payment *because it saves thousands of dollars in interest costs.* By having it in a separate account, he can quickly refer to it and know whether he has sufficient funds for his next car.

PAY YOURSELF FIRST IS AN IMPORTANT LAW OF EMPOWERMENT!

This insight was shared with me by a woman who took my Money 101: A Breakthrough Seminar for Women. She called me several months after the workshop and said, "Donna, Pay Yourself First has been such an easy principle to apply to my financial life that I suddenly realized it could work just as powerfully in other aspects of my life. Finding time to exercise and pray during the day has been a constant challenge. It dawned on me several weeks ago that I should apply the Pay Yourself First principle to everything in my life that is important to me"

"That's what I have been doing, and it works! Before I leave my house, I take time to exercise and have a quiet time to pray and meditate. Then I am focused and in control of my life for the day. My energy has increased and I feel great about myself! Pay Yourself First works in areas other than money."

Experiment in your own life.

> **FIRST THING IN THE MORNING:**
> Spiritual: Pray and meditate
> Physical: Exercise
> Health: Eat breakfast, drink water and take your vitamins

WHY IS PAY YOURSELF FIRST SUCH AN IMPORTANT LAW OF EMPOWERMENT?

First, it is about taking care of business. Make sure what needs to be handled is, in fact, handled efficiently and effectively.

Second, because once you leave the house and get out into the world, life grabs hold and swings you hither and yonder until you return at the end of the day exhausted, ready for the comfort of home, and much too tired to care about your spiritual, physical, financial, or general health. Take care of priorities first. Then relax and enjoy your life.

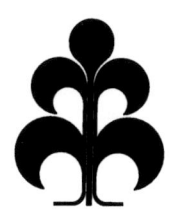

One of my favorite "$12.50 per week" stories was told to me by a bellydance student. In 1975 when she told her husband she was pregnant, the very next day he opened a mutual fund for college expenses. By the time the baby girl was 12 years old, there was sufficient money to send the child to four years of college! The loss of the $12.50 per week had not even been noticed after the initial first few months. The $12.50 per week that they continued to invest became a nest egg for the future.

Pay Yourself First makes sure those things you dream of can, in fact, become a reality.

A WORKSHEET FOR YOUR FIRST STEPS TO FINANCIAL FREEDOM

Where can I find $12.50 per week to invest for my financial future? Consider spending less as an opportunity rather than a burden. Make it a fun game. Be proud of every nickel you save and sing the song "The pennies just piled up one by one." Track your spending for a week or two and observe where you can save a dollar or two by the simple change. It does not have to be a dramatic shift in life-style to squeeze out $12.50 per week.

EATING OUT: Take lunch to work. Gather for potluck with friends rather than going to an expensive restaurant.

MOVIES AND VIDEOS: Check out from the library. Buy tickets in bulk. Go in the afternoons when the prices are cheaper. Watch PBS and discuss the program with family and friends.

BOOKS AND MAGAZINES: Check out from the library. Recycle by sharing magazines with friends. The absence of magazines helps to keep the house neater.

FAST FOOD, COFFEE AND SNACKS: We spend lots of money in this area. You understand the power of compound interest and know that $12.50 a week can be worth $9,000 in ten years. Is that $5.00 coffee and muffin worth it? Weight loss is another advantage to eating fewer snacks.

LOOSE CHANGE: Put it in a jar and watch the pennies pile up one by one.

CLOTHES: What to do when we love clothes so much? Remember a dress costs you hours of work. Is it worth it? Can you be happy with another less expensive one IF you put the difference in your fund to create financial independence?

This system does not work if you sacrifice something and then don't bother to invest the $12.50 per week on a regular basis. In order for this program to be successful, you must set up a mutual fund and automatically have the $12.50 per week ($50.00 per month) deducted. Consistency is the key to success.

If you save $1.79 in the seven areas listed, you will have $12.50 toward your mutual fund. Isn't this fun?

REPETITION CREATES ABILITY

PAY YOURSELF FIRST is the key to creating financial security for your future.

DEPOSIT MONEY from your paycheck into your investment account for financial independence before paying any other bills.

THE SIMPLE SECRET of the financially secure individual is . . .

PAY YOURSELF FIRST

What Is The Eighth Wonder Of The World?

COMPOUND

INTEREST

Chapter Two

What is the Eighth Wonder of the World?

LET'S BEGIN WITH $12.50 PER WEEK
at 9%:

Deposit $12.50 per week for 10 years in a piggy bank, you will accumulate $6,000.

Deposit $12.50 per week for 10 years in a mutual fund that returns 9%, you will accumulate $9,675.

Deposit $12.50 per week for 20 years in a piggy bank, you will accumulate $12,000.

Deposit $12.50 per week for 20 years in a mutual fund that returns 9%, you will accumulate $33,394.

Deposit $12.50 per week for 30 years in a piggy bank, you will accumulate $18,000.

Deposit $12.50 per week for 30 years in a mutual fund that returns 9%, you will accumulate $91,537.

Compound Interest

ISN'T THIS FUN? LET'S CONTINUE WITH $12.50 PER WEEK AT 12%

Deposit $12.50 per week for 10 years in a piggy bank, you will accumulate $6,000.

Deposit $12.50 per week for 10 years in a mutual fund that returns 12%, you will accumulate $11,502.

Deposit $12.50 per week for 20 years in a piggy bank, you will accumulate $12,000.

Deposit $12.50 per week for 20 years in a mutual fund that returns 12%, you will accumulate $49,463.

Deposit $12.50 per week in a piggy bank for 30 years you will accumulate $18,000.

Deposit $12.50 per week for 30 years in a mutual fund that returns 12%, you will accumulate $174,748.

After 30 years, wouldn't you rather have $174,000 than $18,000? Learn how to invest so you can live a life of financial security.

Albert Einstein, when asked what was the most fascinating mathematical formula in the world replied, "compound interest." Now that you understand the magic of compound interest, don't you agree with Einstein?

The previous pages reveal the power of investing $12.50 per week over 10 years and 30 years. Some women say to me, "I have more than $12.50 per week, and I am ready to invest it!" The following chart ("The Financial Warrior's Table" on page 24) is included to encourage you to invest more as you feel comfortable and confident. Your confidence increases as you become more knowledgeable. Knowledge increases as you read and study and take money seriously. Applied Knowledge is power!

Compound Interest

My cousin Mark, a mathematical genius and a CPA with an MS in Statistics, created the following chart for me when I first started teaching about money. Most charts are too complicated and confusing. He designed a simple, easy-to-read version.

What is the purpose of this chart? To show you how much money you will have at the end of a certain number of years (depending on how much you invest each month and the return on your investment). It will inspire you to invest each month. Remember...

CONSISTENCY IS THE KEY TO SUCCESS

What is the Eighth Wonder of the World?

"The Financial Warrior's Table"

Yearly 10 yrs.   20 yrs.   30 yrs.   40 yrs.   50 yrs.

	10 yrs.	20 yrs.	30 yrs.	40 yrs.	50 yrs.
6%	163.879	462.041	1004.515	1991.491	3787.191
9%	193.514	667.887	1830.744	4681.320	11669.102
12%	230.039	989.255	3494.964	11764.773	39058.341

1. Select the row by choosing an appropriate interest rate (6%, 9% or 12%).
2. Select the column by choosing the time of investment (10, 20, 30, 40, or 50 years).
3. The row and column determine the annuity multiplier in the interior of the table. (For example, 193.514 is the annuity multiplier for 10 years at 9%.)
4. Multiply this annuity multiplier by the amount invested each month. (For example, $50.00 a month times 193.514 equals $9,675. This is the amount of money you would have after 10 years of investing $50.00 per month at 9%)

Compound Interest

You may be the fortunate woman who can invest $125 per week ($500 per month). Let's calculate $500 per month for 20 and 30 years at 9% return.

Follow the instructions under
"The Financial Warrior's Table"

$500 per month at 9% for 20 years is calculated by multiplying
$500 × 667.887 (annuity multiplier).= **$333,943!**

$500 per month at 9% for 30 years is calculated by multiplying
$500 × 1830.744 (annuity multiplier)= **$915,372!**

THIS IS ALMOST A MILLION DOLLARS!

What is the Eighth Wonder of the World?

For most women today an adequate retirement is an issue of grave concern. The United States government offers its citizens the opportunity to invest in the stock market (or other less volatile options such as Certificate of Deposit - CD) through an Individual Retirement Account (IRA) which has special tax advantages. An IRA is a financial instrument that permits you to invest up to $4,000 per year ($333 per month which is $83.25 per week).

Follow the instructions under "The Financial Warriors Table"

$333 per month at 9% for 20 years is calculated by multiplying

$333 x 667.887 (annuity multiplier)=

$222,406

For 30 years the result is $609,637
For 40 years the result is $1,558,879

Isn't that amount of money at the end of 30 or 40 years worth setting aside $83.33 per week (or $11.90 per day)?

Compound Interest

When I began my 1000 mile journey to become a Financial Warrior, I was frightened and overwhelmed with zero confidence in money matters. This chart was pivotal in transforming my attitude toward investing money and my ability to handle finances. Many times during the middle of the night I would wake up in a panic, terrified that I was going to be remembered, not as my high school's first female Student Government President, but the first graduate to become a bag lady! With no money or knowledge, the future looked bleak.

THE "FINANCIAL WARRIOR'S CHART" CHANGED THAT PERSPECTIVE.

I would get out of bed, run over to my desk, grab the calculator, and figure one more time what $12.50 per week would be in 20 years. The amount was so astounding to me that it comforted and inspired me to invest more. Each month I decided to "give up" something. The first month I sacrificed two fancy coffees and $5.00 was added to my investment portfolio.

> **WHAT A DIFFERENCE $5.00 MAKES!**
>
> $50.00/month at 9% for 20 yrs = $33,394
> $55.00/month at 9% for 20 yrs = $36,733

<u>Your Money or Your Life</u> by Joe Dominguez & Vicki Robin profoundly influenced my life. They pointed out that the cost of a product is a dollar amount, but it represents hours of work and one's life force. The question is not how many dollars does the silk blouse cost. The question is how many hours of my energy, my precious life, will I have to work to obtain the object of my desire? Is it worth it?

The next time you want to spend money, think carefully. How many hours of my life is the item worth? If the answer is yes, it is worth x hours of my life force, then spend joyfully. If the answer is no, then either do not buy it or invest the amount joyfully for the future.

REPETITION CREATES ABILITY

According to Einstein,
what is the most fascinating
mathematical formula in the world?

COMPOUND INTEREST

Consistently, month by month, invest $50.00 ($12.50 per week) or $100.00 every other month to create . . .

FUTURE FINANCIAL SECURITY

Where Do I Put My Money So It Can Grow?

MUTUAL

FUNDS

Chapter Three

WHAT IS A MUTUAL FUND?

My definition of a mutual fund is: pooling your money with a group of people so you can invest in stocks and bonds with as little as $12.50 a week and get the advantages the wealthy have always enjoyed--professional management and diversification!

A dictionary definition of a mutual fund is a financial organization that pools the money of its members to invest it in a variety of stocks and bonds (called securities). The fund does not have a fixed amount of capital stock but sells additional shares to investors as the demand requires.

For $12.50 per week it is not possible to find a professional to "manage a portfolio." However, if 20,000 individuals put $12.50 per week into a mutual fund company, you have one million dollars. For one million dollars you can hire a professional to manage the portfolio and to diversify the investments.

HOW DO YOU DECIDE IN WHICH MUTUAL FUND TO INVEST YOUR MONEY?

Number One

Go to your public library to study *Consumer Reports*. *Consumer Reports* is a respected magazine dedicated to protecting the consumer, Ms. J. Q. Public. An article evaluating mutual funds is published each year in the spring. This report reviews mutual funds and ranks them. It is one of the easiest and quickest ways to learn basic information about the mutual fund world. After selecting several mutual funds in the top ten ranking in *Consumer Reports*, do more research in *Morningstar*.

Number Two

Learn to read *Morningstar*. *Morningstar* is an independent publication whose purpose is to evaluate and rank mutual funds. It is a daunting undertaking in the beginning, but you can learn to decipher it. I will teach you how to read the report after a discussion about basketball and mutual funds.

Consider the analogy between mutual funds and basketball teams. In North Carolina this comparison is easily understood because basketball is a statewide passion.

If you were to predict a winner in basketball, you would consider Chapel Hill (Michael Jordan's alma mater) or Duke. Why? Because for as long as anyone can remember these teams win the most basketball games. Why do they win games? The coaches are good. They know how to pick basketball players and put together a winning team.

FOLLOW THIS STRATEGY WHEN PICKING YOUR MUTUAL FUNDS!

Look at mutual funds that have a proven track record. Have they been "winning" i.e. producing good returns on their investments for ten years? Good returns to me are averaging at least 10% per year over 10 years since that is the stock market's historical position. If they perform better, that's great. But, as an educated consumer, I am happy with a 10% return.

Check out the fund manager, the "coach." He or she picks the "players," the stocks and bonds, and combines them into a "'winning team" - your portfolio. Since I am investing for the long term, a mutual fund manager must have a ten year track record for me to select him. Ten years is my comfort zone; I want to know that the fund manager "coach" is consistent. I may be a bellydancer and Sahara-traveling adventurer, but when it comes to my money, I am conservative.

Each person is different. It depends on your personality, the amount of time you have to invest, the amount of money you are willing to risk, and other factors. After you have studied and are an educated consumer, it is a good idea to select a financial advisor to review your strategy and discuss options.

SOCIALLY RESPONSIBLE FUNDS

Do you worry about how your money is being used to create wealth? If so, you may want to examine mutual funds that select stocks and bonds based on their beliefs as well as the annual average return.

Socially responsible investors put their money where their hearts are. You may select funds that refuse to buy stocks in companies that sell weapons, liquor or tobacco, discriminate in race or gender, employ sweatshop or child labor, or profit from gambling. Refer to *Consumer Reports* annual equity mutual funds report to find rankings and phone numbers.

A web sight to learn more is:
www.socialfunds.com

Where Do I Put My Money So It Can Grow?

INVESTING IN INDEX FUNDS

In March 1998, *Consumer Reports* referred to investing in index funds as "investing on cruise control." Why? Index funds may follow the Standard & Poor's 500 index (S P) , Wilshire 4500 index, Russell 2000 index, or a variety of international index funds. You won't get the roller coaster thrill of the highest returns, but neither will you suffer the agony of the roller coaster drop to the lowest. According to *Consumer Reports*, the index funds often outperform actively managed funds. To learn more about index funds, check *Consumer Reports'* spring issue. Rankings of their favorite selections and phones are listed.

Mutual Funds

Although investing in stocks and bonds through mutual funds is less risky than investing in single stocks, it is still volatile and risky. However, if you have ten years to ride the roller coaster, it can be profitable. The stock market is like walking up a staircase playing with a yo-yo. The yo-yo is the stock market that goes up and down and the accomplishment is in climbing the stairs slowly but surely. At the end of the climbing you are at the top of the stairs. At the end of ten years, even with the yo-yo "stock market" going up and down, you have a higher return on your money than most other places you could invest it.

Remember, past performance is no guarantee that the team will win in the future. However, it is an indicator that someone is doing something right, whether it is a basketball team or a mutual fund.

Where Do I Put My Money So It Can Grow?

HOW TO READ MORNINGSTAR

Ask the librarian for assistance in locating *Morningstar*. The following is a simplified description of where to find information on the 8 1/2 x 11 page devoted to each mutual fund. There is lots of data, but I am highlighting only the basic points we discuss on pages 39 - 43. You can learn how to read the other sections as the need arises.

| Mutual Fund Name | 2. Load |

| 1. Historical Profile Stars |

| 6. Portfolio Manager |

| History 4. Total Return% |
| 3. Expense Ratio% |

| Performance 5. Trailing 5 yr. avg. 10 yr. avg. |
| 7. Sector Weightings |

1. STARS - At the top of the page evaluating a mutual fund is a box labeled *Historical Profile*. Inside are the words Return, Risk, Rating with one, two, three, four, or five stars. *Morningstar* rates mutual funds with stars. I only consider mutual funds with three, four, or five stars. *Morningstar* evaluates thousands of mutual funds; this, at least, cuts the field down. My experience is that *Consumer Reports'* top-rated mutual funds are three, four, or five stars.

2. LOAD - At the top of the page is a column labeled LOAD. A mutual fund is called LOAD or NO LOAD depending on the fees charged. I only consider funds that say "none." i.e. NO LOAD. A LOAD fund states the sales commission (example 5.75%). When the column says "Closed", it means they are not accepting new investors at the moment. Keep an eye on the best performing ones; sometimes, they reopen for new investors.

Whether it is a LOAD or NO LOAD, a mutual fund is a business that charges a fee for its services just like any business. It's in the business of buying and selling stocks and bonds (called securities), and the goal is to make as much money as possible. Expenses for running the business such as rent, utilities, phones, and salaries are deducted from the mutual fund earnings before the mutual fund investors (you and me) are given any profits (called dividends and capital gains).

<u>NO LOAD mutual funds charge a fee for operating expenses and the rest goes back to the mutual fund investors.</u> When you invest in a NO LOAD mutual fund, you are responsible for phoning the company to request the prospectus and filling out the paperwork. The folks who answer the phone are very helpful in assisting you to fill out the form, but they do not give investment advice. However, all of your money is invested and goes to work for you. No sales commission or load's is taken out.

Mutual Funds

<u>LOAD mutual funds charge a fee for operating expenses plus a sales commission. The sales commission is called a "load."</u> When you invest $100, as much as $8.50 can legally be taken out as a sales commission. Therefore, only $91.50 may be going to work for you. The advantage is that you have an investment advisor to discuss options, make suggestions, and fill out the paperwork.

Which are better - LOAD or NO LOAD mutual funds? After researching *Consumer Reports* and *Morningstar*, I chose NO LOAD. If you feel more comfortable with an investment advisor, then LOAD funds would be a better fit.

Whether a mutual fund says LOAD or NO LOAD, avoid other charges: 1) the annual 12b-1 for marketing expenses, 2) a contingent deferred sales charge levied if you sell within a certain amount of time. It often decreases to nothing if you hold the fund five years, and 3) the back-end load charged when you sell your mutual fund. The back-end never goes away.

3. EXPENSE RATIO - On the right side of the evaluation sheet under "History" are listed 13 factors used in analyzing the mutual fund. You can read the history of the mutual fund year by year from 13 different angles. Expense Ratio is number 10, and <u>I consider only mutual funds that charge 1.50% or less per year.</u>

4. RATE OF RETURN TotalReturn% - Look under the "History" section. The second line reads Total Return %." The mutual fund must perform an average annual return of 10% for at least 10 years to be selected by me. This line allows you to check the returns each year of the funds life. The stock market has averaged 10%-11% over the past 75 years. For beginner long-term investors, a 10% return on your investment is realistic.

5. RATE OF RETURN-Trailing - On the left side of the evaluation sheet under "Performance" is listed "Trailing." It records the three, five, and ten year "Total Returns." It verifies that the mutual fund has an average annual return of 10% over ten years.

6. FUND MANAGER "COACH"

- On the left side of the evaluation page is a section "Portfolio Manager." The fund manager's education, experience, and time with the mutual fund company are described. My requirement is that she or he must have at least ten years of experience with the mutual fund company. The exception is if she has been an outstanding stock picker with another fund and is a new member of the team. Sometimes mutual funds have several managers; it honors the tradition that two heads are better than one.

7. SECTOR WEIGHTINGS

- Look at the lower right section "Sector Weightings." This lists the % of stocks in utilities, energy, financials, industrials, durables, staples, services, retail, health, and technology. The general opinion is that a fund should have no more than 33% in one sector of the economy. It is a "don't put all your eggs in one basket" way of thinking. There are, as always, exceptions to the rule. But for the beginner mutual fund investor, the 33% sector weighing rule is a good idea.

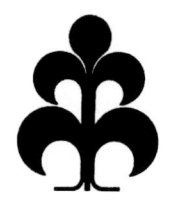

Today it's easy for me to say "just call and get moving," but I still remember how frightened I was when I picked up the telephone to ask for an application for a mutual fund. And the fear was there even before that moment.

The first time I went to the library and looked at the wall of books about finances, waves of nausea swept over me. My knees went weak and my stomach churned. Do not fear. You can learn what you need to know about mutual funds by reading *Morningstar*, investigate individual stocks and bonds, or anything else you decide to do. You can do whatever you choose to do. This book is your first step in the thousand mile journey.

Mutual Funds

    The first time I phoned a mutual fund company to request an application, I was scared to death. However, the people who answered the phones are the nicest folks in corporate America, in my opinion. They were happy to answer my questions and acted as if they had all day to talk with me. When my young son called, they congratulated him on being such a young investor and assisted him every step of the way.

    Stay focused. If a bellydancing mamma can do it, you can too. In summary, when you study *Morningstar*, check the following points:

STARS - must have 3, 4, or 5
NO LOAD - EXPENSE RATIO of 1.50% or less
RATE OF RETURN - 10% for ten years
MUTUAL FUND MANAGER - 5 or 10 years
    experience
SECTOR WEIGHTINGS - no more than 33% in
    one sector.

Remember why I suggest investing in mutual funds rather than in individual stocks. A mutual fund offers to the small investor advantages that wealthy investors have.

1. Enough money to hire a professional who buys and sells securities

and

2. Enough money to diversify and, thus, reduce the risk.

Congratulations!

You are now ready to call the mutual fund company of your choice, fill out the papers, and start dollar cost averaging today!

REPETITION CREATES ABILITY

*Visit your local library

*Read the *Consumer Reports'* annual article rating mutual funds

*Select five mutual funds to study

*Read the *Morningstar* evaluations of these five mutual funds

*Choose one mutual fund

*Start investing $12.50 per week

What Is Dollar Cost Averaging?

CONSISTENCY

IS THE KEY

TO SUCCESS

Chapter Four

DOLLAR COST AVERAGING

A dictionary definition of dollar cost averaging is investing a fixed dollar amount at regular intervals. My definition of dollar cost averaging is to invest $12.50 per week ($50.00 per month or $100.00 every other month) over a long period of time. I'm defining "A Long Period of Time" as a minimum of ten years. For those of us who do not want to follow the stock market daily and worry about the ups and downs, dollar cost averaging is the way to go. Each month have the money automatically transferred from your bank account to your mutual fund.

The nature of the stock market is that the prices of stocks and bonds go up and down. One thing you know for sure, next week or next month the market will either be up or down. Dollar cost averaging is a technique for catching the highs and lows of the market so the price ends up being an average of all purchases. By investing the same amount at regular intervals, you sometimes buy

What Is Dollar Cost Averaging?

more shares and sometimes buy fewer . . . and end up with an average cost. You must be willing to invest long term (minimum 10 years) for this theory to work. *However, as a teaching example, look at this three month situation:*

Invest $50.00 each month

* The first month the price per share is $5.00, you buy 10 shares

* The second month the price per share is $2.50 a share, you buy 20 shares.

* The third month the price per share is $3.75, you buy 13.3 shares.

At the end of three months you have purchased 43.3 shares. The 43.3 shares at $3.75 per share are worth $162. Your investment is $150.00 ($50.00 per month for three months). You have earned $12.00 more than you spent.

This is an example of why dollar cost averaging works...some shares were purchased at a high price, some at a low price and some were purchased at a medium price. In the end, dollar cost averaging is a technique for catching the highs and lows of the market and ending up with an average price. It is almost impossible to predict what days prices are going to be high or low (called "timing the market"). Therefore, it is best to consistently invest each month on the same day and not worry about it. Research shows that dollar cost averaging is a dependable way to invest in the stock market.

Don't we all love a sale? When stock prices are low you are getting your shares on sale. Over the long term the high prices and low prices will average out and you will be spared the agony of trying to "time the market." Most financial advisors agree that "timing the market" is risky business and cannot be done consistently.

For beginning investors, consistency is

the key to success. Dollar cost averaging is the simplest and easiest strategy. So, each month, rain or shine, good times or bad times, invest. Start with $12.50 per week ($50.00 per month or $100.00 every other month) and soon you will be inspired to invest more and more.

> Consistency Is
> The Key To Success!
>
> Remember:
> Consistently investing $12.50 per week
> ($50.00 per month) for
> 20 years at 9% equals $33,000
> and
> 30 years at 9% equals $91,000
> and
> 40 years at 9% equals $234,000.
>
> Dollar cost averaging . . .
> Investing a fixed amount
> on regular intervals
> over a long term.

Consistency Is The Key To Success

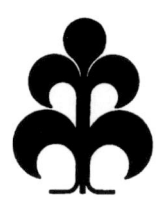

Dollar cost averaging is like catching the wave in surfing; you cannot guarantee that every time you jump on the surfboard the wave will be great. By trying over and over you average out some good waves, some bad waves, and overall a good ride.

The same is true of investing in the stock market. No one can guarantee you the best day to invest your money. But if you consistently invest month after month, you will catch some good days, some bad days, and have an overall good average return on your investment. This assumes that you did your homework and invested in a good performing mutual fund.

REPETITION CREATES ABILITY

Dollar Cost Averaging is investing the same dollar amount at regular intervals over a long period of time.

Dollar Cost Averaging is a way of investing your money in the stock market. More shares are bought when prices are low and fewer shares are bought when prices are high. This technique keeps the purchase price an average over a period of time.

Consistency is the key to success.

What Is The Silent Thief?

INFLATION

Chapter Five

What Is The Silent Thief?

INFLATION

A dictionary definition of inflation is a continuing rise in the prices of goods and services. Inflation eats up the value of your money a little bit at a time year after year. Inflation is the silent thief that steals your money.

How much did it cost to go to the movies when you were a kid? I saw Tarzan in 1950 for nine pennies. Today in Greenville, NC it costs $7.25.

What will it cost to go to the movies in:
- 10 years — $11.82
- 20 years — $19.22
- 30 years — $31.32
- 40 years — $51.05
- 50 years — $82.99

*Based on an average annual 5% inflation rate
AARP Money Management Workbook For Women

Inflation

In 1975 Kacem and I rented our first house in Greenville, NC for $125.00 a month. Today, the same house rents for $550.00 a month.

What will it cost to rent this house in:

10 years	$977.00
20 years	$1,591.00
30 years	$2,593.00
40 years	$4,224.00
50 years	$6,888.00

In 1972 when Kacem and I were first married, we lived in Berkeley, California. We purchased gas for our 1952 green Chevrolet truck at the corner of Shattuck and Vine. We paid $ .29 a gallon regular price and $ .19 on sale. Today we purchase gas in Greenville, NC for $2.50 a gallon.

What Is The Silent Thief?

What will it cost to buy gas in:

10 year	$4.88
20 years	$6.63
30 years	$10.80
40 years	$17.60
50 years	$28.68*

Each year goods are more costly.
The price goes up.

In 1978 a stamp cost $ .06.
In 2006 a stamp costs $ .39.

In 1978 cigarettes cost $ .33 a pack.
In 2006 a pack costs $4.00.

In 1978 a loaf of bread cost $ .23.
In 2006 breads costs $2.50.

What will a stamp, cigarettes, and a loaf of bread cost in 10, 20, 30, 40 or 50 years?

Inflation

Does your salary keep up with the increase in the price of everything? A salary of $24,000 today will need to increase to $63,000 in twenty years just to maintain the same life style!!!! What is the biggest risk to your financial future? Doing nothing. DO NOT PROCRASTINATE.

Why is the biggest risk to your financial future doing nothing? Because your money will lose value as the years pass. It will take more money to purchase the same product. To protect your purchasing power you must act!

PROTECT YOUR MONEY FROM INFLATION

The purchasing power of $1.00 in 1925 is $10.00 today. It takes $10.00 today to buy what $1.00 would buy in 1925.

If you had invested $1.00 in 1925:
Treasury Bills would be worth $17.00 today
Government Bonds would be worth $51.00 today
Blue Chip Stocks would be worth $2,279 today
Small cap Stocks would be worth $7,860 today

Source: Ibbotson-Morningstar

REPETITION CREATES ABILITY

What is the Silent Thief?
INFLATION

Inflation eats up the value of your money a little bit at a time year after year.

What is the biggest risk to your financial future?
DOING NOTHING

If you do nothing, each year inflation (the Silent Thief) will slowly but surely steal the purchasing power of your money.

What Is Diversification?

DO NOT PUT

ALL YOUR EGGS

IN ONE BASKET!

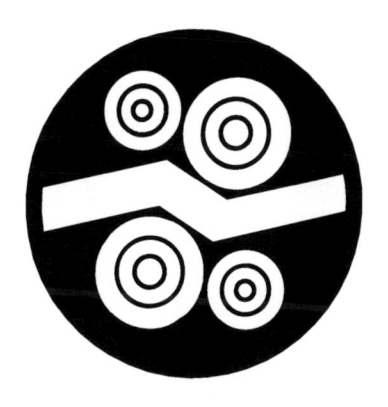

Chapter Six

What Is Diversification?

ALL YOUR EGGS?????

Folk wisdom is the distilled knowledge of human experience. Do not put all your eggs in one basket! You heard that wise saying in your childhood; it has stood the test of time. How does it relate to financial independence and financial planning?

"Do not put all your eggs in one basket" means to diversify your money. If you drop one basket, you have eggs in other baskets so you won't starve.

It's the same idea with your money. Your investments need to be divided among different financial "baskets." Because the stock market is so volatile, which just means it goes up and down in price, you do need other investments than stocks. Stock market statistics over the last

Do Not Put All Your Eggs In One Basket!

100 years reveal that if you buy a good performing group of stocks and keep them 20 years, they will increase in value 9% to 10%. *The stock market has historically outpaced inflation.*

Choose stock mutual funds for long term goals such as retirement and college.

Choose certificate of deposit or the money market for shorter term goals such as saving for a house or building an emergency fund.

Choose to invest in rental property. No matter what happens to the stock market, people have to have a place to live.

What Is Diversification?

Because the stock market is volatile, a portfolio needs more investments than just mutual funds. The definition of portfolio is the stocks, bonds, or other securities held by an investor. Both my children have designed their retirement programs. Adam started investing in mutual funds at age 11 and Farah Lisa at age 18. They are now prepared to diversify. My advice is to invest in a duplex after they finish college. Why pay someone rent when you can buy, live in one side and rent out the other side to help pay the mortgage?

Rental property is another basket to invest money.

Do Not Put All Your Eggs In One Basket!

What other financial instruments i.e. "baskets" should I consider? Invest in different kinds of mutual funds so you can catch the *ebb and flow* of the stock market.

Sometimes value funds are performing well.

Sometimes growth funds are performing well.

Sometimes large cap funds are performing well.

Sometimes small cap funds are performing well.

Sometimes bonds are performing well.

What Is Diversification?

The purpose of this book is not to go into detailed explanation of stocks and bonds. The book list in Chapter 10 is provided for further study.

My goal in writing this book is to start you on the journey of becoming an educated consumer. A thousand mile journey begins with one step.

REPETITION CREATES ABILITY

Do Not Put All Your Eggs
In One Basket

Diversification Is Dividing
Your Money Into
Different Investments
So As To Get The
Best Return And
The Most Protection

Who Can Help Me
Put It All Together?

HOW TO CHOOSE A FINANCIAL PLANNER

Chapter Seven

CHOOSING A FINANCIAL PLANNER

Why do you need a financial advisor? Not everyone does, but if you want to consult with an expert to verify your plan of action, you need to select a financial planner carefully. Choosing a trusted financial counselor to guide you in deciding into what baskets to invest your hard-earned money is a very important decision. As an educated consumer, you now understand the power of Paying Yourself First and Compound Interest. You are now committed to creating financial independence for yourself. The next step may be to select a financial advisor.

Ask your friends, family, banker, lawyer, minister, and doctor for a recommendation. If the same name keeps coming up, that is an indication the individual is respected and trusted in your community. But don't stop there.

Who Can Help Me Put It All Together?

Attend the free seminars various financial institutions offered in your city. These are marketing evenings for them; they want to educate the public about investing, planning for the future, and of course, to convince you they can do it best. In these classes you can ask specific questions you need answered. You can also find out what information a financial planner will need in order to evaluate your particular situation.

DON'T FORGET. The purpose of a financial planner is to <u>assist</u> you in designing your financial future, not to take it over. Do not look at having a financial planner as relinquishing your power to make decisions that affect your life. One purpose of writing this book is to educate women to make their own decisions. There is no shame in seeking advice and assistance. Do not be afraid. You are capable of learning how to handle your finances.

Qualifications of a Financial Planner

After you are prepared to consult with a financial planner and know the information she will need, it is important to inquire about her credentials. All financial planners must pass a standard exam. Some choose further study and obtain additional credentials. Experience and certification are important.

- * Three to five years of experience
- * CFP Certified Financial Planner or
- * ChFC Chartered Financial Consultant

These designations require course work and high ethical standards. To stay licensed, the financial planners are tested and must attend 30 hours of classes every two years.

Call the <u>Institute of Certified Financial Planners, 800-322-4237</u> to ask for a list of local members.

Cost of a Financial Planner

Financial planners may *be* paid either by fee only, commission only, or a combination of the two. There are two types of fee based planners. One charges by the hour. The other charges a percentage of the assets that they manage for you. The more money they make for you, the more money they make for themselves.

Some financial planner's income is tied to the commissions they receive for selling financial products. It can *be* considered a "conflict of interest." On the other hand, fee only advisors can *be* expensive. Either way, it is a legitimate expense for you *because* you are buying people's knowledge.

Remember the "Rule of Three"

1st   **3rd**

2nd

Ask three financial planners the same questions about your financial situation and compare the responses. This rule works in life whether asking for directions or comparing insurance policies. I learned about this technique when studying an American Association of Retired Persons (AARP) money management class. These are in-depth financial education workshops for women. Please contact AARP in Washington, DC 601 E. Street, NW, Washington, DC 20049 (1-888-687-2277) to learn of a seminar near you. It is mentally and emotionally challenging, but well worth the time, energy, and money.

REPETITION CREATES ABILITY

*Educate Yourself
*Read Financial Books
*Attend Seminars and Classes

Select A Financial Planner
Based on Credentials, Experience,
Reputation, and
How Much They Charge!

Remember . . .
A Financial Planner's purpose is
to <u>assist you</u> in designing your
financial future!

How Can I Change My Attitude Toward Money?

QUOTES

TO

LIVE BY

Chapter Eight

QUOTES TO LIVE BY

Do you remember the day you realized you would have to take responsibility for the future financial well-being of your family? It could have been because of divorce, widowhood, or your spouse's refusal to do so. Either way, the abject terror is paralyzng. Where to go? What to do? Who can help ?

Repeat these words to yourself:

I CAN DO IT

WOMEN CAN DO ANYTHING THEY WANT TO

WOMEN CAN MANAGE THEIR MONEY

Religion and psychology agree that affirmations possess the power to transform a person's life. Today, in one second, you must commit to switching your attitude, thought patterns, and feelings about money. Who has time and money for years of therapy? Stand up, turn around, declare

"I Am A New Woman About Money!"

Repeat to yourself daily.

I Am A Financial Warrior

Money Is My Servant Not My Master

I Am Interested In Money

I Am Fascinated With Money

I Am Inspired By Money

I Am Successful With Money

Money Is Fun

Money Is An Adventure

Money Energizes My Life

Money Is My Friend

How Can I Change My Attitude Toward Money?

What helped me to overcome my paralyzing fear of money? Looking at *books* about money created waves of fear and nausea. I didn't want to read them. All the 80's and 90's self-help books talked about your mind being powerful, so I decided to test the theory.

I would connect money that I hated and dance that I loved and in the process transform my attitude about money. I LOVE to dance. For years, I have taught "belly" dancing. I grew up "shagging" on the southern beaches. Dance is in my blood. My strategy was to connect money topics with dance movements.

When I opened up a book about money, rather than going to sleep or my eyes glazing over, I said to myself "What fun it is to shimmy!" I would jump up from my desk and dance around the house listening to music and shimmying. It sounds strange but it worked. Dancing taught me mutual funds. I read a paragraph about mutual funds and danced a soft sexy chiffi-telli. I read a paragraph about dollar cost averaging and swirled into a veil dance.

Give it a try. You have nothing to lose but your fear of learning about money. What brings pleasure into your body creates a view of the world. Associate pleasure and learning about money and you have conquered the first step in a 1,000 mile journey to financial independence.

Words have a powerful effect on our bodies and our energy so choose words to strengthen you!!!

Each person must select the positive statements that inspire and choose a physical activity that associates pleasure with learning about money. You must do this if you want to succeed and have fun learning about money.

> My favorite affirmation is:
> I live a simple and elegant life.
> Doesn't that sound like more fun than living a frugal life?

REPETITION CREATES ABILITY

Words Have

A Powerful Effect

On Our Body And Our Energy.

Choose Words

To Strengthen You!

Practical Tips For Life

SIMPLE AND

IMPORTANT

THINGS TO KNOW

Chapter Nine

INFORMATION TO KNOW

♥ "Gratitude is the memory of the heart" (French proverb). Be grateful for what you have. It is the foundation of a happy life.

♥ Memorize poetry and scripture while walking or exercising.

♥ Shop around for credit cards. Compare cards interest rate, grace period, late fee, and annual fee.

♥ Take naps and eat a good breakfast.

♥ When a new bank opens up in town, check it out. Often they offer free checking to the first 100 customers, if you're 50 years old, or some other gimmick.

♥ When you gain five pounds, lose it! "A minute on the lips, forever on the hips."

Simple and Important Things To Know

Add one payment a year to your house mortgage. Divide it by 12 and add that amount each month and have it applied to the principal. Why? It saves you a lot of money in interest. For example:

> Regular monthly payment for a $75,000 loan at 10% is $658.18.
>
> Divide $658.18 by 12 = $54.85.
>
> Add $54.85 to the regular payment $658.18 = $713.03.

End up saving $57,000 and cutting 9 years off the loan.

Look for the "coffee factor."" A couple wanted to save money but not change their life style drastically. They cut out the coffee and muffin they picked up on the way to work and saved $1,200 per year. Look for these kinds of savings in your life.

$1,200 invested each year at $100 per month for 20 years at 9% becomes $66,788. Isn't that fun to know? Check my calculations on page 24, the Financial Warrior's Chart.

Check out the deductible on your car insurance. It is possible to double your deduction from $250 to $500 and cut your insurance premium. Putting the amount you save on the lower premium into a special savings account is the key to this strategy. If you do have an accident, the $500 deductible is in an account. If you do not have an accident, the $500 is earning interest for you.

Always have a car payment. Why? It means that you never have to borrow money to pay for a car except the first time. By pretending that you have a car payment, even after your car is paid for, you gradually save that amount each month. Put this money in a special car savings account until there is enough to pay CASH for your next automobile.

Consider buying a used car. The largest drop in the value of a car i.e. depreciation occurs in the first two years. In 30 years of marriage, we have never paid more than $5,500 for a vehicle.

Simple and Important Things To Know

● Have you ever thought about getting a mortgage for your house for 19 years rather than 15 or 30? It never crossed my mind that you could borrow money for anything less than what the banker offered . . . 15 or 30 year mortgage. In fact, you can. Ask for a computer print out showing the payments from 15 through 30 years. A mysterious mathematical event occurs around 19 years. The payments are not that much more than the 30 year ones. It is an option you need to know exists; it gives you more choices. This principle can be applied to borrowing money for anything.

● Should I pay off all my debts before starting to invest? Many financial advisors encourage people to do this. It did not work for me. If I had waited to pay off all my debts, I would have become so discouraged, I would never have started to invest. My suggestion is to start investing $12.50 per week in a mutual fund and pay $12.50 per week toward eliminating your debts.

Exercise for 10 minutes each morning before you leave your bedroom. Simple stretches and the yoga "Salute to the Sun" are my favorites. Pay yourself first applies to your physical and financial well-being. Once you leave the sanctity of the bedroom, life grabs you, swings you around, returns you home at the end of the day exhausted and not excited about exercising. In my experience, maintaining good health and proper weight depends more on exercising for short periods of time on a regular basis than exercising for a long time sporadically. Consistency is the key to success. A little exercise every day echoes Lao Tzu's advise . . . "Little drops of water wear away the largest stone."

Simple And Important Things To Know

REPETITION CREATES ABILITY

Be Grateful For What You Have

Make An Extra House Payment Each Year To Significantly Reduce Your Mortgage

Always Have A Car Payment

TAKE CARE OF YOURSELF

What Do I Do Now? Homework

A THOUSAND MILE JOURNEY BEGINS WITH ONE STEP

Chapter Ten

START TODAY

Deposit $12.50 In A Special Account TODAY!!!

✔ As you begin the 1000 mile journey to financial independence, you must study to develop the confidence to invest in mutual funds, real estate, art, gold, or whatever suits your needs and personality. Set a goal of one year or less to educate yourself. Until that day, start putting $12.50 per week into a savings account. Pay yourself first is a good habit to develop. Read, study, and soon you will be confident enough to invest.

Read *Consumer Reports* and *Morningstar*

✔ *Consumer Reports* publishes an article evaluating mutual funds each year. *Morningstar* is an independent publication whose purpose is to evaluate and rank mutual funds. Both can be found at the public library.

What Do I Do Now? Homework

Make an appointment with your company's personnel officer.

✓ Ask "How much will I receive the day I retire from this company? What will my health coverage be? How much will it cost to cover my family?" Find out where you stand as soon as possible.

Call Social Security Commission
1-800-772-1213
www.socialsecurity.gov

✓ The Personal Earnings and Benefit Estimate Statement is now being sent to you without your requesting it. You may have thrown it away. If so, call the above number to request another one. You will discover how little you are going to receive from Uncle Sam. Social Security was never meant to be a pension plan. It was designed as a safety net to keep the elderly from starvation. You will need your company's pension plan, your own investments and Social Security to create a comfortable retirement.

Study

☑ Attend any classes offered in your community about financial planning and investments. Look in the phone book yellow pages under INVESTMENT SECURITIES, MUTUAL FUNDS, STOCK AND BOND BROKERS. Many investment companies offer <u>Free</u> classes. I find them to be very informative; financial advisors are often excellent teachers. Sometimes the seminars include free meals. Call the local community college and university to check on classes. These classes may charge a tuition.

Ask Family and Friends

☑ Ask family members and friends what they know about investing. You will be pleasantly surprised. Aunt Martha who makes quilts and pecan pies may turn out to be a hot shot mutual fund, stock or bond picker. Never judge a book by its cover. I discovered a millionaire housewife in the library in the reference section reading *Morningstar*. Learn what you can from everyone you encounter and always follow up with your own research!!!!!

✓ Read! Read! Read!
and listen to audiotapes

My favorite book is <u>The Wealthy Barber</u> by David Chilton. It is fun and easy reading and has the best explanation of dollar cost averaging.

<u>The Richest Man in Babylon</u> by George Clason explains that the principles of creating wealth are ancient and yet applicable to modern times. It is fun and easy reading.

<u>Money Doesn't Grow On Trees</u> by Neale S. Godfrey and Carolina Edwards is my favorite for raising financially responsible children.

Jane Bryant Quinn, Peter Lynch, and Suze Orman write excellent books. Their style is reader friendly.

MAGAZINES: *Money, Kiplinger, Fortune*
NEWSPAPERS: *Wall Street Journal, New York Times, Barron*
NEWSLETTERS: Bottom Line/Personal,
P. O. Box 50379, Boulder, Co. 80323-0379

REPETITION CREATES ABILITY

Start SAVING $12.50 per week TODAY!

Read financial books and magazines

Attend financial classes and seminars

Start INVESTING in a mutual fund with your $12.50 per week Savings within one year!

IN CONCLUSION

What becoming powerful about money has created in my children...

Adam was 11 years old when I sat him down on the red rust sofa one rainy Sunday afternoon to teach him *Money 101: A Breakthrough Seminar for Women*. My bellydance students had asked me to teach them what I had learned about money. It had taken me months gleaning my class notes for the points that had impacted me the most. When I learned these simple concepts they transformed my life.

Now I was using my sweet 11 year old son as a guinea pig. "If an 11 year old boy can understand these six points then anyone can," I theorized. "Adam do you have $6.25 to set aside for building your financial future? If you do, I will match you $6.25 per week which makes $12.50, and we can start you on the road to riches."

Conclusion

After an hour of playing "The Financial Warrior's Table" game, he was hooked. He started a neighborhood business "Adam's Lawns and Ponds." Each week he mowed lawns, weeded flower beds, fed cats, walked dogs, picked up newspapers and mail for weekend vacationers. He even designed and dug a small lily pond with the help of his Dad.

He was taking his first step on the 1000 mile journey to financial independence. The bank down the street welcomed his business. We opened a checking and savings accounts. Checks were printed with two lines so he and I could sign. The tellers teased him that he would be the first student they knew who could balance a checkbook. From the age of 11 until 16 we invested $12.50 per week ($50.00 per month).

In 1997 at the age of 16, we stopped investing in the mutual fund. At that moment we had invested $3,000 simply by depositing $12.50 per week ($50.00 per month x 12 = $600 per

Conclusion

year) for five years. If Adam never adds another penny to the $3,000, based on a 9% average annual return, this $3,000 will be worth $223,050 by the time he is 66 years old. For a young man who desires passionately to be a jazz pianist, this is important information. He must design a financial plan for a secure future. Musicians and other artists are challenged because rarely do they have work that provides retirement benefits. Now he understands it does not take a lot of money; however, it does take consistency in investing a small amount.

When Adam was a sophomore in college, he made an offer to buy the duplex he was renting. He went to a realtor, filled out the offer to purchase, paid earnest money, and discussed a loan with a bank officer. The deal did not go through, but he was practicing the steps he will need one day to be an educated house buyer. At 19 I was practicing my shag dance steps. It never crossed my mind that I could be investing in property.

Conclusion

Adam has choices I will never have. We have calculated that the $3,000 left in the account to experience the magic of compound interest at 10% will be worth $352,170 at 66. If he chooses very wisely and gets a 12% return, it will be worth $897,000. I do not have 50 years. Well, maybe I do. But, it is better to begin when you are 20 rather than 60. The concepts of paying yourself first and the magic of compound interest work for everyone, but they are magic for the young. The sooner you start the better.

Farah Lisa, six years older than her brother Adam, was a senior in high school when we sat down to learn about creating financial freedom. At the time her allowance was $40.00 a month. This amount covered her gas and spending money. She was responsible for any additional expenses. Her jobs consisted of baby-sitting and practicing the violin with young children. This special time was called "play practice" and parents were willing to pay high school students to inspire their budding violinists.

Conclusion

Contributing $25.00 per month was more than half of her allowance. It was a significant commitment from a 17 year old. However, Farah Lisa immediately understood the Tim and Tom story (see p. 4) and agreed to invest $25.00. Several months later, she said, "Mom, I do not miss the $25.00 I pay myself first because I have added new "play practice" partners to replace that money." Realizing that one adjusts spending habits to what one earns was an important lesson. It always remained in Farah's mind. Even when she was a college student working as a waitress, she invested $50.00 a month in her mutual fund. Today as an adult, it is a basic principle of life that she pay herself first. She, too, will be a much wealthier woman than her mother as a result of this knowledge.

Learning about money and teaching your children about money are great gifts to yourself and to them. Freedom and power exist in our lives when we put money in its proper place.

Conclusion

The joy and excitement of learning about money and writing this book came from an amazing realization. It is a simple process. It is simple, but not easy. Compare it to eating right. You learn that in order to lose weight and maintain it, you must eat a balanced diet, drink water, and exercise. The directions are simple. But it is not easy to discipline yourself to do so.

The same is true in the world of creating financial security and independence for yourself. You now know that in order to create financial independence, you must pay yourself first and invest consistently each month at least $12.50 weekly ($50.00 a month). The directions are simple. Disciplining yourself to do so is not always easy. The key to success is commitment. Once you understand the basic formula for creating financial security, then bend your will to your mind. Anyone can find $12.50 a week to invest in her future financial independence if she wants to do so.

Conclusion

All my life I had been terrified, fearful, and resentful of money. Once I made my mind up to overcome this nonsense, the fog began to clear. Yes, it did take several years of reading, going to classes, and asking friends and family for help before I had the courage to do anything. Finally, I did have the information and the courage to begin investing. Today, I am in a much happier space financially and emotionally in relationship to money. The journey has been worth it for me and my family.

I treat investing in the stock market with the same awe and respect that I tackled crossing the Sahara Desert. In 1972, Kacem and I married and decided "to retire." My observation was that folks worked hard all their lives so they could retire to travel and enjoy life. Often the reality was they were either too sick or one of them died. My Aunt Helen told me when she retired, "I have the time and the money to travel the world, but, I do not feel like crossing the street." Without children, mortgage,

Conclusion

and insurance premiums, we were free spirits to wander the world. So we did.

We decided to visit West Africa. I studied African folk dance at the University of Ghana and Kacem studied with a local sculptor Korbla Sakpaku. Being young and adventurous, we decided to drive across the Sahara Desert to Ghana.

Before we started our 6,000 mile journey, we read books about adventurers who had gone before us, talked to a Frenchman who had just returned, and made a list of what was absolutely necessary to take in case anything went wrong. Of course, what went wrong for us was the one thing no one we knew had experienced.

That which is fun, profitable, and significant in life holds an edge of danger. The challenge is to enter each event with a shield of knowledge, a sword of preparation, and a helmet of faith that you have done your best - and enjoy the experience.

Conclusion

Crossing the Sahara Desert is like investing in the stock market. One must read and study the books of those who have gone before you, talk with the ones who are recently involved, make a list of what you think is necessary to do it, have faith you have done your best, and enjoy the trip!

Now I enter the library to read *Consumer Reports* and *Morningstar* and decide what is the best mutual fund to invest my hard-earned money. One day I might be brave enough to invest in single stocks, but for the moment I am a mutual fund devotee. It offers me professional management, diversification, the least risk, and a minimum of paper work.

Conclusion

Experience shows that if
you pay yourself first
and invest a fixed amount each month
over a long period of time
(dollar cost averaging)
in a mutual fund,
you *will* reap the rewards
of a consistent investor and *be*
financially independent long before you ever dreamed.
START TODAY !!!

GLOSSARY

STOCK is the value of a business, divided into portions called shares of uniform amount, which are represented by transferable certificates. The holder of one of these is a <u>part owner</u>.

BOND is a certificate issued by the government or private company which promises to pay back with interest the money borrowed from the payer of certificate. The holder of one of these is a <u>lender</u>.

INDIVIDUAL RETIREMENT PLAN (IRA) is a personal retirement savings plan for anyone who is employed. ROTH IRA is a variation that may suit your needs better. Consult a financial advisor.

SECURITIES are stock or bond certificates.

MUTUAL FUND is a financial organization that pools the money of people to invest it in a variety of securities (stocks or bonds). The fund does not have a fixed amount of capital stock but sells additional shares to investors as the demand requires. Mutual funds offer professional management and diversity to investors both large and small.

Glossary

CERTIFICATE OF DEPOSIT (CD) is a written acknowledgment by a bank that it has received from the individual named a certain amount of money as a deposit. The interest rate is determined by the length of time the money stays in the bank. The return on the investment is usually lower than stocks and bonds because there is no risk You will receive the amount you deposited plus the agreed interest

STOCK MARKET-is a place where stocks and bonds are bought and sold. The New York Stock Exchange is most famous one.

STOCK INDEX (INDICES) are indicators used to measure value changes in stock groups that represent different segments of the economy. The following are often quoted: STANDARD AND POOR'S 500 (S & P), DOW JONES INDUSTRIAL AVERAGE, NASDAQ.

401K is a retirement savings plan with tax advantages. Employers may offer matching funds. Ask your personnel officer for details.

529 COLLEGE SAVINGS PLAN - a program for funding educational opportunities.

About The Author

Donna Whitley is a lifelong resident of Greenville, North Carolina--except for the time she studied at Woman's College (now the University of North Carolina at Greensboro), worked for the honorable Senator Sam J. Ervin, Jr, in Washington, D.C., and the National Conference for New Politics in Chicago, and traveled across Europe and the Sahara Desert. Married to Kacem Sebti, son of a Moroccan Ambassador, whom she met while in Morocco bellydancing in a nightclub, her proudest achievements are her marriage and the rearing of Farah Lisa and Adam. They are young adults who her friend Mary described in her newspaper column as "...loving, intelligent, talented, creative, cultured, well-mannered, and kind individuals." Donna agrees.

About The Author

For over 30 years, Donna has taught belly dancing. For 20 plus years she has been a Mary Kay Consultant. Presently, Donna is teaching *Roadmap to Riches on $12.50 Per Week*, a companion seminar to her book, at colleges and in private workshops. The Dance of Life: A Business Devoted to Empowering Women Through Classes in Money, Movement, and Make-up is the umbrella organization.

These businesses enabled her to stay at home with her children and be an active volunteer in local politics, PTA, and church. Her passion for travel has taken her to West Africa and China to study dance, Cuba and Vietnam on work mission visits, and Morocco to enjoy family and fun.

Since her children graduated from high school, Donna's energy has been devoted to writing this book. Her commitment is to educating women in America and the world about how to become financially independent.

Donna Whitley teaches a companion course *Roadmap To Riches on $12.50 Per Week: First Steps To Financial Freedom* worldwide.

For further information regarding a speaking engagement in your community, contact her at:

Donna Whitley
1800 Forest Hill Drive
Greenville, NC 27858
email: donna@donnawhitley.com
To purchase books, go to amazon.com or www.donnawhitley.com

She would love to hear from you.